To, Jean + Bob Swensen
with best wishes

from:
Mary Howard + Don

10/6/79

PRAYERS

PRAYERS
Disturbance and Transfiguration

Donald Houston Stewart, D.D., Ph.D.

Donald Houston Stewart.

10/6/79

Exposition Press   Hicksville, New York

First Edition

© 1978 by Donald Houston Stewart

All rights reserved, including the right of reproduction in whole or in part, in any form or by any means, electronic or mechanical, including photocopying, recording, or by any information storage and retrieval system. No part of this book may be reproduced without permission in writing from the publisher. Inquiries should be addressed to Exposition Press, Inc., 900 South Oyster Bay Road, Hicksville, N.Y. 11801.

ISBN 0-682-49153-5

Printed in the United States of America

Contents

Foreword
    Prayers—Magna Cum Laude   7

Preface   9

A Prayer for Humility	11
A Prayer for Those Who Are in Distress of Soul	12
A Prayer for Steadfastness	13
A Prayer of Confession	14
A Petition for a Lively Worship	15
A Personal Prayer	16
A Prayer of Thanksgiving for Inspiring Spirits	17
A Marriage Prayer	18
Private Prayers	19
A Prayer for Discipline	21
A Prayer for Dedicated Living	22
A Prayer for Daily Living	23
A Prayer for Personal Commitment	24
An Intercessory Prayer	25
A Prayer for the Nation and World	26
A Prayer for the World, Our Home	27
Prayers in Thanksgiving	28
A Congregational Prayer	30
A Prayer for Holy Week	31
A Prayer for the United Nations and Its Purpose	32
A Prayer for the United Nations and Its Responsibilities	33
A Prayer for New Lives in a New Year	34
A Prayer for Spiritual Strength	35
A Prayer for Overcoming Serpents in the Garden	36
A Prayer for Daily Guidance (I)	37
A Prayer for All Who Work	38
A Prayer for Changed Life-Style	39
A Prayer for a New Year (I)	40

A Prayer for the Betterment of Civil Life	41
A Prayer for Courage to Change the Structures of Society	42
Some Private Prayers and Petitions	43
A Prayer of Thanks for God's Sacrament of Disturbance	47
A Prayer for Daily Guidance (II)	48
A Prayer for Faithful Living	49
A Prayer for the Strength to Choose Aright	50
A Morning Prayer	51
A Litany of Thanksgiving and Confession	52
A Prayer for Deliverance (I)	53
A Prayer of Thanksgiving for Life's Little Sanctities	54
More Prayers for Daily Living	55
A Prayer for Deliverance from Uncharitableness of Spirit	58
Two Evening Prayers	59
More Morning Prayers	60
A Prayer for Sensitivity to God's Presence	62
A Prayer for Deliverance (II)	63
A Prayer in Praise of the Lord's Blessings	64
A Prayer That We Be Saved from Ourselves	65
A Prayer for Strength in the Face of Life's Adversities	66
A Prayer for Deliverance from Debasing Fears	67
A Prayer for Daily Guidance (III)	68
A Prayer for a New Year (II)	69
A Prayer for Daily Guidance (IV)	70
A Prayer for the Grace to Strengthen Others	71
A Thanksgiving Prayer	72
Two Vesper Prayers	73
A Prayer for Daily Strength	74
A Prayer in Thanksgiving for Love and Friendship	75
A Prayer for the World's Workers	76
Commencement Prayers	77
A Prayer for Convocation Day	79

Foreword

Prayers—Magna Cum Laude

At long last, a book of prayers that deserves the accolade —Magna Cum Laude. My ecumenical ministry over a twenty-year period in Metropolitan St. Louis brought me into the Sunday worship services of hundreds of churches of all denominations: Protestant, Catholic, and Jewish. It was a rich, rewarding, and privileged experience, allowing me to hear great scholarly preaching and also poor, unprepared pulpit pounding. Often I was reminded of Mark Twain's remark: "We went away with that indefinite sense of being filled but not fatted." And sometimes I escaped by remembering haiku: "My ears had found the sermon dull and stale; but in the words outside—the nightingale!"

When it came to the Pastoral Prayer, my most frequent response was: "Pardon me, your theological slip is showing." Over the years of my involvement in worship services in a wide spectrum of traditions, I found an abysmal lack of theological integrity. The person doing the praying would begin by addressing God and would soon be talking to God about God, mixing metaphors, moralizing, memorializing names and causes, and ending all in Jesus' name—a church commercial with something for everybody.

Whenever I had a free Sunday, I rejoiced to go to First Presbyterian Church, Kirkwood, where one of this generation's great preachers was fulfilling a scholarly, socially-sensitive servanthood. Donald Stewart's preaching was biblical, brilliant, brave, and therapeutically related to our human condition. His prayers were theologically sound and interiorly nurturing. They were vehicles for conveying the good news that life can be new—your life, my life, and the life of the world.

What a privilege that, at long last, the public can experience these prayers in this book of Magna Cum Laude Prayers.

—*O. Walter Wagner, D.D.*
Former Director of the Metropolitan Federation
of Churches, St. Louis, Missouri

Preface

My own conviction is that all prayer is the human creature's awareness that he or she is both addressable by and answerable to the Creator, the providence and ground of one's being.

Public prayers are intended to awaken the hearer to the Creator's query: "Where on earth are you, Adam (man)?" Their purpose is to call forth a creative response to a questing Lover.

These prayers were called into being by those who heard them. The verbalizing of prayer has always been harder for me than that of the sermon. I only hope that they may "awaken" now, as I hope that they did originally.

I dedicate these prayers to the people of the congregations I have served: Dixon Memorial Church U.S., Tarrant City, Alabama; The First Presbyterian Church U.P.U.S.A., Frankfort, Kentucky; Central Presbyterian Church U.P.U.S.A., Houston, Texas; and The First Presbyterian Church U.P.U.S.A., Kirkwood, Missouri.

I submit them in the hope that amid our deep concern for the peace of the whole world we shall not overlook or belittle the lives which we live one by one.

—The Author

A Prayer for Humility

Bestow upon us, O God, a lively sense of humor.
Save us from the folly of conceit. Enable us to see how ridiculous we are when we try to strut.
Enliven us with the spirit of heavenly laughter, so that we can recognize our own failures and imperfections, without resentment.
Deliver us from posing as paragons of virtue, lest people expect of us that which we cannot possibly deliver.
Strengthen us to have done with the spirit that is glad when others go wrong, lest we be no longer shocked at our own sins.
Teach us to rejoice in the successes of all wholesome ventures.

    From all ugliness of spirit, Good Lord, deliver us.

Amen.

**A Prayer for Those
Who Are in Distress of Soul**

Grant Thy healing power and presence, O Lord,
    Upon all who sorrow, or are distressed in spirit and mind;
    Upon all anxious, defeated, and troubled souls;
    Upon those everywhere who seek forgiveness and
        restoration,
        Who hunger for enlightenment and communion with
        Thee;
    Upon us all, bestow again the authority of Thy Holy Spirit
    and the Peace of Thy communion with us.

Begotten in Thy Light, deliver us from all darkness.

Lifted by the powerful tide of Thy creative purpose,
save us from all despair and loneliness.

Pour out upon us the Power of Thy healing purpose,
so that knowing ourselves created afresh by the
dominion of Thy Love, our hearts may be in our time
the cradle of Thy coming again in transforming power.

    Through Him who liveth and reigneth with Thee,
               world without end,

                                    Amen.

A Prayer for Steadfastness

O God, who in Thy wisdom hast prepared for each of us our tasks to do for Thee, give us, we pray, such honesty and perseverance that we may seek to fulfill Thy will for our lives, serving where we are needed.

Enlighten the perplexed, strengthen the fainthearted, rouse the indifferent, and kindle in us the spirit of true devotion, so that in the hour when Thy summons calls we may be strong to do Thy bidding.

Let it so be, O God.

Amen.

A Prayer of Confession

Hear us, O Lord, as we make our humble confessions:

We are heartily ashamed that so often we have lived insensitive to our dependence upon Thy gracious providence, new every morning and fresh every evening.

We confess our repeated acts of willful self-indulgence whereby we have wasted the substance of time and talents which Thou hast divided to us;

Have mercy on us, our Father, for all in us that dims our knowledge of Thy Grace, makes us stumbling blocks to others, leads to the arrogance of self and forgetfulness of Thee.
We humbly pray Thy forgiveness and restoration.

Create a clean heart and renew a right spirit within us, we beseech Thee, that we shall no longer mar the beauty of Thy creation by our selfish living.

Let this be in truth our fervent prayer.

Amen.

A Petition for a Lively Worship

Reclaim us, O Lord, as we come to worship:

> We have wandered afar, lost our name, forgotten our features, and know not who we are.

> Let loose the creative ministry of Thy Holy Spirit in our souls as we wait before Thee;

For all who worship here this day,
> May life become greater for any who have been contemptuous of it;
> Simpler for those who have been confused by it;
> Nobler for those who have tasted its bitterness;
> Sterner for those who have assumed the ease of it;
> and Holier for all whose lives have been threatened with the loss of all dignity, beauty, and meaning.

Through Jesus Christ, our Lord,

Amen.

A Personal Prayer

We confess before Thee, our Father, our manifold sins
   against Thee and our brethren.

Save us from the futile quest to escape the discipline
   of Thy laws that sustain and enliven our cities and
   countryside.

Forgive us that we have so often diminished life's demands;
   By treating minimums as maximums;
   By accepting the mediocre as the excellent;
   By imagining that slovenly work is acceptable;
   By posing as allies of Thy purpose while we
     obstruct the path of Thy righteousness.

From all faulty imagination, lack of affection for
  the Good, and weakness in willing the Good—
From all such
            Deliver us, we beseech Thee, O Lord.

                                          Amen.

**A Prayer of Thanksgiving
for Inspiring Spirits**

    We give Thee thanks, our Father,
        for all those who, passing this way before us,
        have beautified the highway of our earthly
        pilgrimage with the splendor of their lives;

        For all who have turned the commonplace into
        the Holy of Holies; who have lifted the burden
        of the weary and spilled the fragrance of their
        lives to sweeten the scene of our human anguish;
                              We give Thee thanks.

  As we partake of the inspiration and strength which
their lives have bestowed upon us, their younger
brethren, let the remembrance of them rest as a
living benediction upon all our days, so that in our
days we too may be the ministers of light and
strength, peace and comfort.

                      So let it be, O Lord.

                                Amen.

A Marriage Prayer

(To be used at the close of the ring ceremony)

O Thou who art the giver of all life and love,
Bless with Thine own happy benediction
These lives now one, who first met life as two.
May the Love which Adventures be their
        unfailing Inspiration;
May the Love which is Constant be their
        invincible Strength;
May the Love which Understands be their
        abiding Peace;
May the Love which is Complete be their
        abounding Joy.

                Through Jesus Christ, our Lord,

                                  Amen.

Private Prayers

I

Almighty God, who committed to us the swift and solemn trust of life, since we know not what a day may bring forth but only that the hour for serving Thee is always present, awaken us lest we be unaware of the instant claims of Thy Holy Will.

Consecrate the hours of our days with Thy Presence, so that in weakness or in strength, in sorrow or in joy, we may find our lives transformed and guided by the Power of Thy Grace.

Through Jesus Christ, our Lord,

Amen.

II

I so often get in my own way, O Lord.
    I dawdle away precious hours doing nothing that matters.
    It is so easy to float on the stream of others' activities.
Startle me lest I become a burden that others must carry.
Teach me to recognize the talents with which Thou hast
    blest me.
Lead me to put all that is in me into the living moment.
When I am wrong give me the grace to acknowledge it and
    to learn from my inadequacies.
When I am right make me easy to live with.

I thank Thee for the many inspiring persons who have
    influenced and helped to mold me.
    Make me of some creative help to all whom I meet,
    especially those in my own home.

        So let it be, O Lord, from this day forward.

                                          Amen.

A Prayer for Discipline

    For spirits that have been greedy for power
to satisfy our own uncleansed desires;

    For hearts that have loved too well the chief
places in the eyes of men;

    For the iniquity of the serpent within us
whereby we have practiced deception and insincerity
in thought, word, and deed;

    For all guile whereby we have deliberately sought
the defeat or the frustration of those we have been
pleased to call our friends—

    For the manifold and unsuspected wickedness of
our hearts—
        Forgive us and cleanse us, O Lord.

                                  Amen.

A Prayer for Dedicated Living

Open Thou the doors of our souls to Thine entrance.
  Come in, O Lord, today; come in to stay.
Give us the attentive ear that we may hear aright Thy
  call to obedient service:
Create in us a receptive mind that we may welcome the
  light of all new knowledge.
Endow us with sensitive hearts, swift to discern Thy
  coming upon us to enlist us in Thy purpose:
Bless us with ready hands, cleansed spirits delivered
  from all meanness and littleness that we may be
  faithful and generous stewards of all with which
  Thou hast entrusted us for a season.

  Grant that it may be so throughout all our days.

Amen.

A Prayer for Daily Living

Deliver us, we pray, from belittling the life we are called
   to live from day to day.
In the hours of despondency, when we are tempted to neglect
   the task of the moment, because we can make no sense in
   things that go to pieces, deliver us, lest we default in
   life's ordinary duties by which we are trained for
   greater stewardship.

When life is dark and the road steep and rough, enable us
   to remember that this life of ours has been divinely
   lived, that this robe of flesh and strange infirmity
   was once upon a time Thy garment.
Lead us, we pray Thee, to become more than conquerors
   through Jesus Christ, our Lord.

                                              Amen.

A Prayer for Personal Commitment

Almighty God, who hast made all ages a preparation
   for Thy Kingdom,
      Move us to present our hearts to the Dominion of
      Thy Royal rule;
      Let not the bluster, the fears, and the confusion
      of this world's perplexities cause us to forget
      from whence we come, where we serve, and whither
      we go in Thy purpose.

      Give us the wisdom to read aright the signs of
      the times.

      Suffer us not to forget the bond that unites us
      with the pain and anguish of our fellowmen and
      women throughout the world.

      We confess all sins we have most grievously committed
      against Thee, our fellows, and ourselves from time to
      time.
      Grant us Thy forgiveness and renewal as we make our
      individual confessions:

          (period of silence)

Now send us forth strengthened to fulfill the tasks to which
   Thou hast called us one by one.

                  Through Jesus Christ, our Lord,

                                   Amen.

An Intercessory Prayer

We invoke Thy strengthening grace,

> For all who are this day faced by great temptation;
> Upon all who stand in the valley of decision;
> To all who are suffering now the consequences of
>   sins long since repented of;
> For those who by reason of an early environment
>   never had a fair chance;
> For all whose family circles have been broken
>   by death;
> For all teachers who labor to lift high the lamp
>   of truth in lonely and faraway places;
> Upon all who work to make this world a better place
>   in which to work and live.

Grant the blessing of Thy companionship,

        Through Jesus Christ, our Lord,

                Amen.

A Prayer for the Nation and World

In this time of troubles, grant wisdom and courage, patience and vision to all our leaders, O Lord.
Inspire with Thy Spirit the President, the Vice-President, all Members of Congress, and the Governors of our States, and all in positions of trust and responsibility in our land.

May deeds of righteousness, justice, and mercy so reign in our land that harmony and peace, freedom and learning and compassion shall fashion our people as a community of concern and love.

Save us from the evil where the strong ignore the weak, tread upon the powerless, and make a mockery of justice because it is in their power to do so.

So save and transform our land, O Lord.

Amen.

A Prayer for the World, Our Home

We lift up before Thee, our Father, the nations of the Earth.

Amid awakenings to opportunities undreamed of by our fathers, save us all from repeating the sins of the past on an even greater scale.

From greed, hatred, and the will to seize the "lion's share" of the world's resources, deliver Thy creation, O Lord.

Deliver us from playing with Thy world through the instruments that science has developed, lest too late we find ourselves on the road to catastrophe.

Teach us so to appreciate one another that we shall forsake confrontation for reasonable deliberation to make this earth a good habitation for those who shall come after us.

Make us loyal to these intentions
through Thy Holy Spirit.

Amen.

Prayers in Thanksgiving

I

I thank Thee, my Father:

For the gift of life. I have nothing that I
did not receive at Thy hands:

The life that stirs within me;
   The bright and beautiful world of nature;
For the smell of earth after rain;
   For the scented air of mown hay;
For gardens and flowers,
   fun, sun, and scudding clouds;
For the live community of persons;
   For the inspiration of friends and
      the lift of love that rescues me from myself.
For music and books, good company;
   For work to do and the strength to do it;
For all the wholesome pleasures of this world
   which Thou hast made

Let me now express my deepest thanks to Thee.

Help me to adorn this gift of life while I am still
among the living.

So let it be, O God.

Amen.

II

O Thou who art the restless recreator of our souls,
we gratefully remember:

> Thy powerful and steadfast purpose of reconciliation;
> Thy Love that seeks us even when we have given up on
> ourselves;
> Thy faithfulness that abides amid all our faithless
> living;
> Thy Grace that accepts us, unacceptable as we are;
> Thy Love's surprise in calling sinners to take part
> in Thy purpose;
> The surprise of Thy mercy that alone disarms the entire
> arsenal of our defiant ambitions;

For these and all Thy mercies help us to live in grateful
and obedient response all the days of our years,

To the glory of Thy Name.

Amen.

A Congregational Prayer

O God, who hast begotten us in Thy Love that
we might freely choose to be Thy children:

In all things enable us to draw near to Thee
in spirit and in truth:

As we make our humble confessions
We bring to Thee our *consciences*, so often
marred by our willful disobedience;
quicken them by Thy Holiness;

We bring to Thee our *minds* so often captured
by the trivial and the partial; feed them
upon Thy wholesome Truth, we beseech Thee,
that we may fully know Thee.

We lift before Thee our *imaginations* so often
stained by selfish dreams that have diminished
life's zest:
Purge them by Thy beauty.

We would open to Thee our *hearts* where ungodly
affections so easily dwell;
Fill them with true love of Thee.

We lift up to Thee our *wills* so often weakened by
false choices;
Enliven them with the love of the good, and so
fashion us to Thy Purpose that we may be the sons
and daughters of that health of being which shall
never pass away.

                                                      Amen.

A Prayer for Holy Week

Almighty God, who in Thy Providence hast made all ages
a preparation for the coming of Thy Kingdom:

Deliver us, in this our time, from falling prey to
the delusion that we do so certainly mean what
Thou dost mean;

Have mercy upon us, O God, for Thou alone knowest how
often we have cried Hosanna with the crowd and yet
carried in secret the crown of thorns and the spital of
human disdain for Thy Royalty.

Save us, we pray Thee, from the deception of outward
adoration that hides, even from ourselves, the deep
intent to crucify Thee upon the defiance of
undisciplined intentions.

Defend us, O Master of men, lest we piously forget that
we are one with all the frailties of men who have gone
before us—lest we blaspheme by asking Thy guidance
when we know we have *already* made up our minds to
do what we want to do.

Children of this busy, perplexed, and anxious
generation, save us from ourselves, lest worried about
many things we forget the One thing needful.

                                                    Amen.

A Prayer for the United Nations and Its Purpose

Almighty God, Father of all mankind:

Grant to us and to all Thy children everywhere a new
 will for Thy world made one;
Forgive us our sins of separateness which have kept us
 from Thee and from one another;
Inspire with the love of justice and mercy all who
 represent their several governments in all international
 affairs.
Grant Thy Spirit's guidance and wisdom to all in positions
 of high responsibility in world affairs.

Make us all, as a people, instruments of Thy peace that
 even in these days we may prepare the Highway for the
 Day when Thy Kingly rule shall come, that Thy glory
 may be made manifest in all the earth;

                        Through Jesus Christ, our Lord,

                                        Amen.

A Prayer for the United Nations and Its Responsibilities

Our Father, we bring to Thee our world, tangled and
confused, amid deep anxiety, yet filled with great promise.
Save us from belittling the magnificences of life.
    Cause us to remember with grateful hearts the good things:
        Thy Grace that hath brought us to this hour of high
            demands;
        That life and health, strength and work, love and home,
            fun and laughter are but the vestibule of blessings we
            have for too long taken as a matter of course.
Forgive us for thoughtless minds, ungrateful hearts, and
insensitive spirits that transfigured by Thy Grace we
may live in glad dedication to Thy sovereign purpose
for all mankind.
Save us from the foolish presumption that all's right with
the world:
    Gird our understanding both to see and to feel how our
        selfish discords, hostility to Thy will, and love of
        power over others have sown the seeds of our troubles
        in these present times.
Save us alike from the presumption that all's wrong with the
world:
    Breed in us respect for the principles of life which
        sustain us even against our will to pull Thy laws out
        of plumb.
    Lead us to repentance for the scars we have inflicted
        upon Thy creation and to acknowledge our part in the
        evils of our world.
    Embolden us to deal with deep causes and not with surface
        symptoms that we may live at the center and not at the
        edge of existence.
Satisfy us with the risks of Righteousness that we may join
Thy battle against all evil powers.

                        Through Jesus Christ, our Lord,

                                        Amen.

A Prayer for New Lives in a New Year

So often, O Lord, the days of our years are marred by
   selfish and halfhearted living:
Save us as we embark upon a New Year
   from the tyranny of trifling loyalties that
   neither try us nor give aid to our fellowmen.
Deliver us from being so busy doing nothing of any
   account, while we simply get in the way of
   those who *are* trying to do something worthwhile.
May we not be numbered among those who do the least
   possible in the day which demands the utmost
   of costly loyalty and commitment.
Save us from trying to be the physicians of other
   peoples' ills, lest so busy about others we
   forget our own glaring failures of omission
   and commission.
Grant us the grace of attractiveness of spirit and
   gladness of heart that is always eager to
   believe the best, always gladdened by goodness,
   always slow to expose when others go wrong.
Let us be known in our time as one with those who
   seek the betterment of life and the conditions
   of living for all men everywhere.
So grant us a New World endued with the power and
   purpose of Thy Holy intent made alive for
   all men.

       So let these days attest, O Lord.

                              Amen.

A Prayer for Spiritual Strength

Gracious and Eternal Father, who hast called us into
  Thy service,
    Strengthen us, we pray Thee, to carry out without
    reservations the tasks of the coming days.

  Give to all Thy people the *vision* that can see
  beyond the present;
  The *courage* to undertake the new adventures;
  The *will* to open the road to peace and true
    communication between men and nations;
  The *devotion* to endure the difficult;
  And the *grace* to endure to the end;
That so we may fulfill the vocation to which Thou
hast called us one by one.

Amen.

A Prayer for Overcoming Serpents in the Garden

O Lord, Thou alone knowest how often our good intentions have come to naught through our own misdeeds.
Save us from all that destroys the vines of our life's garden; From cowardice that shrinks from new truth and clings to the familiar because it has been our dwelling place in days gone by, deliver us, we pray.

When we are tempted to stay cozily "at home" in old and established customs of thought and conduct, give to us the faith that ventures with the changeless Truth in a changing world that continually rethinks the mystery of Thy ways with us.

From arrogance that presumes to know all Truth, deliver us, lest we never learn anything.
From the spirit of laziness that is content to ride upon other people's sweat and toil, upon the attainments of those who paid the price for what we inherit, save us, we beseech Thee.
Guard, lest we become so satisfied in comparing ourselves with our fellowman that we forget altogether Thy divine judgment under which we all stand at every moment.

Grant us wisdom so to live, our Father.

Amen.

A Prayer for Daily Guidance (I)

Help us, O Lord, lest we pretend that we are wiser than we are, lest we reveal our ignorance.

Deliver us from appearing busier than we really are, lest men mistake us for someone else and expect from us what we cannot deliver.

Save us from posing as better than we are, lest we be shocked no more by our own transgressions.

Deliver us from all play-acting, lest treating fiction as truth we shall deal with Thy Truth as though it were fiction.

Save us from accepting a little of what we know to be wrong in order to get a little of what we imagine to be right.

In all things when compromises come home to roost and experiences return to plague us, keep us by Thy power from adding to the mistakes of the past that in all our ways Thou mayest direct our paths.

Through Jesus Christ, our Lord,

Amen.

A Prayer for All Who Work

We thank Thee for the many willing hands and the numerous and generous hearts who here do their work in full measure, pressed down and running over, who work, not by the clock, nor by the yardstick, nor yet by the mere letter of the law, but who work because Thy love constraineth them.

O Eternal God, who knowest the weaknesses of men, that we are ever frail about the good, yet ever willful and determined in obstructions of the ways of light, save us from ourselves, we pray Thee, lest we add to the woes of the world.

Save us from using our offices and station in this fellowship as a means for our prestige. Forgive us the hypocrisy that is deaf to the new and the different, not because these are bad, as we profess, but because we know that their adoption leads to the admission that we did not think of them, and that others than those of our own little clique will now lead.

Forgive us, O God, that we are so easily tempted to lord it over others, thus making ourselves such stupid gods. Bridle our tongues, lest we open our mouths only to reveal the empty head, an ugly spirit, or a heart of spite which knoweth not Thee. Suffer us never to forget that the contentious and conceited spirit is the gift that Thou dost bestow only upon little women and petty men. From criticizing the labors of others while we neglect and even mismanage those of our office, deliver us for Thy Kingdom's sake, our **Father.**

Amen.

A Prayer for Changed Life-Style

Save us from the folly that worships at the altar of Self, that looks in its mirror and repeats daily without a qualm the mistakes of every yesterday, from all obstinate refusals to learn our lessons, save us lest haply, while we profess to contend for Thy cause, we be unmasked before the eyes of all save our own, as fighting against the Living God.

Bestow upon us, O God, a lively sense of humor, lest taking ourselves too seriously we shall be unable to see how ridiculous we appear to Heaven and Earth with our haughty looks and our stiff necks. By Thy power save us from becoming serpents who crawl around the garden of Thy Kingdom, seeking whom they may devour, besmirching the good earth with the slime of our envy, or the odor of false witness. Let not the spirit that magnifies or delights in the failures of others, that resorts to the dagger of slander or the rapier of idle and malicious words be so much as known amongst us. Lord, have mercy upon us, miserable offenders.

Pour out Thy Spirit, we pray Thee, upon us.
  Strengthen in every good work the labors of Thy people. Grant Thy richest blessings upon the strangers and all who are new in our midst. The work that Thou hast begun in us, establish Thou it by Thy Power that in all the words and life, in all the work and witness of this people, love and joy, peace and goodness, gentleness and patience, loyalty and faith may be as flowers that beautify Thy Garden.

  Through Jesus Christ, our Lord,

Amen.

A Prayer for a New Year (I)

As now we enter upon new tasks of highways we have not traveled before, enliven us to welcome the new horizons. Give us the power for bigger and more difficult tasks. Save us from temptation to take refuge in the accustomed and familiar.
In all moments of our fears and activities help us to realize that Thou art the God of the New and the Old.

Amid the poverty, and wretchedness, that afflicts our brethren who exist half-fed, ill-housed, unemployed, and wracked by disease and suffering in so many lands and even in our own, open your eyes to *see* what we behold and to *feel* the anguished *word* of silent suffering.

Give us the audacity and the will to effect the changes in the structures of our society that send the weak to the wall while the rich become richer.

Upon our whole earth pour the disturbance of Thy Holy Spirit. Save us from whittling down the demands of Righteousness. In all that concerns the bettering of our habitations on this earth enable us to accept the suffering that we must ourselves undergo in fulfilling Thy will that we shall love our neighbors as we love ourselves.

Make us instruments that shall bring all structures of government and those who serve therein to love mercy, to do justly, and to walk humbly before Thee.

Grant us a New World with our New Year, O Lord.

Amen.

A Prayer for the Betterment of Civil Life

We pray for the life of our nation, its cities, and people, O God.

Help us, our Father, to be creators of opportunities for all persons to bring their full potential to bloom:
Make us instruments of encouragement to those who are looking for a chance to *be*, and to feel that they are truly needed.
To that end give us the wisdom to make our cities places that nourish the hearts and minds, and enrich the lives and homes of our people.

Save us from the desire to accumulate things.
Imbue all who sit on boards and city councils with the determination to make of their communities places where men and women have learned to dream great dreams, and to see noble visions of cities that enlarge people's stature, provide new horizons of attainment, and a wholesome challenge to their residents to run the risks of lofty endeavors that make for creative human fellowship and adventure.

Amen.

A Prayer for Courage to Change the Structures of Society

Strengthen us to build structures of relationships in our human enterprise that will draw out the best in all who partake of their purpose and meaning, so let it be, O Lord.

Bless every endeavor that would create and support dignity; that establishes hope and life; that would open the doors of new possibilities to all those who are being driven to despair, because no one has asked for their services.

Amid the freedom, comfort, and blessings of our land in this time, suffer us not to forget the bond that unites us with the anguish of millions of human beings, young and old, throughout the world.

Teach us so to feel the open sores of the world that we may share more generously what we have, even while we seek to effect the changes in the structures existing of which we are so often the beneficiaries.

Give us the honesty and courage to embody in action what we have here prayed for.

Let it be so, O Lord.

Amen.

Some Private Prayers and Petitions

I

Save me from my own sins and carelessness, my Father.

I confess before Thee,
   Spiteful words and selfish behavior that have
   embittered the sweetness of life.
   Do Thou take control of my tongue.

   I recall failure of self-control that has hurt
   others and marred my own stature;

Enter the citadel of my heart and bridle all my being,
   O Lord, and control the rabble of my city.

Amen.

II

O Lord, I cannot forget that I have put stumbling
blocks in the way of others;
I have obstructed and retarded their progress;

Make me especially sensitive to the well-being
of others; where I can, help me to undo the harm
I have caused.

O God, in the evenness of whose love our divisions
are healed, enlighten me to understand that we are
all the children of Thy one family.

Help me to know that Thou alone art Lord, and so
teach me to give up trying to be in charge of
everything myself.

    Incline me to live the answer to this that I
now pray.

Amen.

III

My Father, so often I have opened my mouth when I
should have kept it shut.
I have more often remained silent when I
should have spoken. Give me Thy wisdom to
commit myself wisely.

Train me, O God, in the art of honest and frank
living that consents to act on behalf of the
good, accepting the cost.

Cleanse my imagination, enlighten my understanding,
that I may serve Thee aright this
day, O Lord.

Amen.

IV

Loving Savior, I have run away from Thee, O Lord,
on the feet of my wayward affections.

Discipline me to love what Thou dost call
me to be and do,
until I love Thee with all my heart,
all my soul, and all my strength and mind,
as Thy grateful child.

Amen.

A Prayer of Thanks for God's Sacrament of Disturbance

For the gift of life with its joys and its sorrows,
For the life of the Spirit with which Thou hast
   endowed us,
For all the hazards of self-declaration which are
   ours in all moments of our choosing,
For pain that follows the love of the low and the
   base,
For the conquest which ensues upon our choice of
   the good and the true,

For all the wholesome evidence that we live and
   move and have our being amid Thy constraining
   grace, that our Life in the Spirit is fraught
   with Thy Disturbance and Thy Love—

For these tokens of Thy daily Grace and Presence,

     We thank Thee, O Lord.

          Amen.

A Prayer for Daily Guidance (II)

O God, who abidest amid the changing, in knowledge of whom standeth our eternal life, grant us that sense of Thy Holy Spirit that in our prayers we shall not ask amiss.

Deliver us from belittling the life we are called to live from day to day. When we are tempted to neglect the task of the moment because we cannot see the distant effect;

When days are dark and despair seems easy, help us to remember that this life of ours has been divinely lived, that this robe of flesh and strange infinity was once upon a time, Thy Garment:

So strengthen us in the Spirit of our Master.

Amen.

A Prayer for Faithful Living

In the hours of high privilege and opportunity;

In moments when the trust and confidence of our fellows have bestowed upon us positions of privilege and power affecting the welfare of countless lives;

Enable us in all such moments to administer honestly and with efficient discretion the opportunities and power thus entrusted to us as the servants of all our people.

<blockquote>So indeed let it be, O Lord.</blockquote>

<blockquote>Amen.</blockquote>

**A Prayer for the
Strength to Choose Aright**

In all moments when the road divides and
our verdict must be given:

> Deliver us, O God, from setting our hearts
>   upon those things that fade at our feet;
>   from all ungodly desires and selfish imaginings;
>   from all that turns the fire of life to ashes.
>
> Save us to the glad abandon of those who follow
>   Thee, not because they must, but because they may;
>   Who choose Thee, with all the kingdoms of this
>   world in sight;
>   Who give their lives away, not because they
>   should, but because Thy love has broken
>   every barrier down;
>
>> Through Jesus Christ, our Lord,
>
>>> Amen.

A Morning Prayer

We thank Thee, our Father, for our creation, preservation, and all the blessings of this life.
   For the firm compulsions of Thy grace that have guarded us against ourselves:
For lessons learned that in Thy providence, darkness can be transformed into light; weakness can be turned to strength; difficulties can become the vesture of high opportunity:
For all Thy mercies new every morning and fresh every evening whereby Thou has taught us that this world is the Arena of Thy "no" and Thy "yes"; of Thy wholesome Judgment and Thy redemptive purpose.
For these and all Thy mercies we give Thee our deepest thanks.
Now gird us anew for the living of these days. From all frailties of sinful self-entanglement that frustrate in us Thy purpose;
   From all futile attempts to escape the discipline of Thy Holy Spirit in the creative revolutions of our time;
   From every temptation to defy the bond that unites us in responsible community with our brethren;
   From every tainted imagination and weakness of will which leads to decisions that disfigure the stature of our being;
   From all debasement of our affections and willful self-alienation from the Good;
   From every seduction that makes us easy prey, deliver us by Thy power, we beseech Thee, O God.
Now create us afresh to be the strong servants of Thy Will in our time.

                        So indeed let it, O Lord.

                                    Amen.

A Litany of Thanksgiving and Confession

Let Us Pray for Forgiveness:
Forgive us, O lord, for the thankless hearts that have taken Thy manifold blessings as a matter of course; for selfish and unseeing eyes that have discerned not our dependence upon Thy providence; for daily acts of willfulness whereby we have wasted the substance of time and talents which Thou hast divided unto us; for all in us, O God, that dims our knowledge of Thy Grace, leads to arrogance of self, and to our forgetfulness of Thee, forgive us we earnestly pray:
    Create a clean heart,
        and renew a right Spirit within us,
    we beseech Thee, through Jesus Christ, our Lord.

                                                  Amen.

A Prayer for Deliverance (I)

Save us, O God, from all vain imaginations
   whereby we caricature the life we are called to live:

   From every device by which we falsify the life of the Spirit.

Deliver us, we beseech Thee:

   From the folly that seeks to create a different world
     with indifferent people;

   From imagining that we can serve Thee with our minds and
     wills while we vote against Thee with our affections;

   From all affectation, untruth, and hypocrisy whereby we act
     outwardly that which we are not inwardly;

   From all stubborn insistence that so weak without Thee we
     are yet so unwilling to belong to Thee;

   From all the weakness of our self-entanglements.

Save us, O Lord, to that glad obedience which wills to do
   Thy will, to love our fellowmen, and to be, in truth,
   the children of Thy Holy Purpose.

                          Amen.

**A Prayer of Thanksgiving
for Life's Little Sanctities**

O Lord, enliven my soul to know Thy Presence all about me—

    For the gift of life, to see the wonders of earth and sky, sea and sun, to feel the raindrops, and the wind.
    For the trust of little children so full of questions, who make me know how careful I must be, lest I pass on my ignorance as truth;
    For love that has known my failings and yet keeps wide open the encouragement of full communion;
    For brave souls that have kept their gentle poise in spite of pain, sorrow, and loss of their body's full vitalities;
    For the inspiration of those around me who are quick to feel the pain, the hunger, the despair of others, and daily give themselves to help heal the wounds of the world;
    For the painful memories of yesterdays, for the achievements of today, and for the hope of tomorrow, transfigured afresh by the power of Thy Grace;
    For all persons and events that have lifted me up, because in them Thou didst call for my obedience;
    For all that causes me to stand in awe, knowing that I live environed always by Thy Sacred Nearness.

For all Thy blessings so richly bestowed, I thank Thee, my Father.

                                                            Amen.

More Prayers for Daily Living

I

When we stand face to face with the choice between desire and discipline, popularity and conscience;

When small acts promise to throw large shadows across our pathway;

In all moments when the tug of betrayal and the temptation of the shortcut looms large;

When the mediocre, rather than the best, would claim our devotion;

In all dividings of the ways, where our verdict must be given;

>Teach us from our heart to pray:

"Thy Will be done now, in this my station, as it is in Heaven.'

>So, indeed, let it be, O Lord.

>>Amen.

II

In the moments of attainment and success, save
us from the pride and illusions of self-sufficiency.

In the hour of weakness and defeat, deliver us, we
beseech Thee, from all self-pity and every
sentiment that so easily unmans us.

Awaken us afresh to the constant overtures of
Thy Holy Will that being obedient to the
same we may come to know the joy of becoming
somewhat the comrades of Thy Holy Purpose,

        Through Jesus Christ, our Lord,

                      Amen.

III

Startle us, O Lord, out of our spirit of complacency,
   lest we become intolerable to all who seek to be
   worthy of life.

   For eyes that looking have seen so little;
   For time received and wasted by loitering feet,
      by self-enclosed minds, and insensitive
      spirits;
   For these and all our miserable sinning against
      Thee and Thy Grace,
                  We pray Thy forgiveness, O Lord.

Teach us so to number our days that we may live as
   those who know that we pass this way but once.

So incline us to apply our hearts unto wisdom and
   our hands to work, that the swift years passing
   may carry with them treasures that neither
   moth nor rust can corrupt, or death destroy,
   because we are partners of the Eternal.

                So let it be, indeed, O Lord.

                            Amen.

A Prayer for Deliverance from Uncharitableness of Spirit

From the disposition that sees the mote in our brother's eye while seeing not the plank in our own eye;

From all narrowness of spirit that detects no significance in the life of our times;

From all that makes us insensitive to the deep meanings of the ordinary and makes us strangers to the costly claims that are being asked of us by Thy Holy Spirit;

From all that would leave us content to exist with little interests and to live as small officials in transient enterprises, while we clutter the earth with our petty demands;

From all such, deliver us, O God.

          Amen.

Two Evening Prayers

Upon the troubled conscience of our generation;
Amid the noise of human fury that betokens the coming night of human impotence and vain expectations:
Pour out Thy Spirit upon all who know that the plumbline of Thy Holy Will cannot be overcome by the wiles of evil men who even in the darkest hours of national and social life bear witness to Thy Holy disturbance and reveal the best even when the day seems to belong to the worst.
Give us courage, Lord, to be always Thy faithful servants—

Through Jesus Christ, our Lord,

Amen.

*   *   *

As we lay down the tasks of this day and commit ourselves to the blessing of sleep in this coming night,
Grant us the rest of forgiven hearts and cleansed consciences.
Awaken us in the coming dawn, ready to live awakened afresh to the miracle of life's daily resurrection.
Help us to live with the audacity and hope which Thou dost give to all who seek Thee;
With the assurance of those who have tasted Thy faithfulness;
With the humility of those who know that we are receivers of Thy Love from start to finish—

So grant us full rest this night, O Lord.

Amen.

More Morning Prayers

I

Almighty God, in whose providence we have been brought to this hour, we thank Thee:

For the gift of life itself;
For the life and Spirit with which Thou hast endowed us;
For risk and venture which attend every moment of our decidings—"to be" or "not to be";
For deep and serious consequences which abide the moments of our choosings;
For the unspeakable compliment of our freedom that makes of life the arena of costly discipline and of costlier disobedience;
For all that tempts us upward through the overtures of the beautiful, the good, and the true;
For all authentic revelation where we have felt and known Thy powerful hand upon our souls;
For every leading of Thy Spirit whereby Thou hast delivered us from the flimsy refuge of the pious reiteration of other people's faith;
For every evidence of Thy daily presence that makes our life an exciting pilgrimage and a luminous event.

For these and all Thy mercies, we thank Thee, O God.

Through Jesus Christ, our Lord,

Amen.

II

Almighty God, now strengthen us to be fully Thy servants in our time:

> From the tyranny of trivial lordships that diminish the magnificence of life;
> From being experts in the things that matter least and from being hollow and empty novices in those things that matter most;
> From being fear-filled souls who misread for the worst every signal of our daily tasks;
>
> From all such, save us by Thy powerful renewal; make us truly the men and women of divine audacity, ourselves the work of Thy new creation let loose in our time for the working of Thy purpose in the world.

We lift up especially before Thee, our Father, all distressed and anxious souls; those who have experienced defeat and who are twisted by guilt; all the troubled, tired, confused, perplexed and the frightened of the world. Upon us all, pour out Thy renewing grace, open our hearts and let loose Thy power afresh in our lives, that Thy Church may become what Thou didst intend it to become—

> Through Jesus Christ, our Lord,

Amen.

A Prayer for Sensitivity to God's Presence

Almighty and Everlasting Father, who alone abidest amid the changing, who alone giveth light amid darkness, as Thou didst visit our fathers before us,

> Grant that we, their children, may know the power of Thy salvation.

Amid the confusion of tongues, give us ears to hear Thy voice, and hearts to love what Thou commandest.

Citizens of a world of strife and suspicion disposed too often to do as we like, create a new heart and a right spirit within us that we may know the joy of serving Thy purpose,

> Through Jesus Christ, our Lord,

> > Amen.

A Prayer for Deliverance (II)

Deliver us, O God, from ourselves—

From thinking that we can persistently mess up our moral arithmetic and then expect life to make some meaning;

From vainly imagining that laziness and indifference can produce responsible persons; that selfishness and greed can add up to a happy community; that suspicion can beget friendship; that deceit and sharp practice can create trust.

From all obtuse folly, Good Lord, deliver us.

Forgive us, O God, that so knowingly we have turned in such absurd arithmetic; save us from the hypocrisy that pretends surprise when our sums are returned to us to do again.

Teach us, Lord, how to be sensible disciples of Thine, lest we be seen as inventions of the devil.

Awaken us to be about our tasks while it is day, lest our pilgrimage be ended before we have begun and we darken the morning of eternity.

Strengthen us to embody what we have just prayed, Lord.

Amen.

A Prayer in Praise of the Lord's Blessings

We thank Thee, our Father—

> For Thy deed of continuing reconciliation;
> For Thy faithfulness that abides all our faithlessness;
> For the unspeakable surprise that Thou dost call even sinful men to participate in Thy Holy purpose;
> For Grace that disarms (with love) the arsenal of our disobedience;
> For the clear revelation that Thou art a God of Judgment *and* of Grace:
> For all Thy blessings bestowed on us,
>> We give Thee thanks;

Now gird us to be truly Thy servants in these turbulent times.
Teach us to tremble at the responsibility of our privilege.
Deliver us from all that diminishes our stature as the children of Thy Grace;

> From all pretense that we can read no meaning in what is happening all around us;
> From pious chatter about "freedom" while we remain silent in speechless fear as evil Powers spew hatred and sow discord, disfigure, distort, and destroy the stature of our fellowmen;
> From all temptation to play at religion—treating Thy Truth as fiction, so that we might serve fiction as if it were truth;
> From all wicked complacency that tolerates for others injustices that we would never allow upon our persons.

Save us from *all* falsification of the life of the Spirit,
> So that: raised by Thy Grace from the death of our self-entanglements, we may live as those who have received Thy gift of power for newness of life.

Through Jesus Christ, our Lord,

                        Amen.

**A Prayer That We Be Saved
from Ourselves**

Save us, O Lord, from ourselves:

> From clamoring for our rights while we neglect our responsibilities;
> From expecting the praise of others, while we secretly delight in the failures of others;
> From harboring grudges;
> From all in us that makes life petty, and mean;
> From all that leads us to diminish life's magnificence and spoiling our human relationships,
>
> Good Lord, deliver us.

Into Thy gracious keeping we commit ourselves, O God. Help us to give Thee sovereignty over our affections, our imaginations, and our wills, so that desiring to serve Thee with our whole being, and our neighbors as ourselves, we may be as towers of strength and courage to those who need us, as ministers of light and comfort to those in dark loneliness.

> Through Jesus Christ, our Lord,
>
> > Amen.

A Prayer for Strength in the Face of Life's Adversities

We thank Thee, our Father, for the adversities through which Thou hast disciplined us:

   For moments of aloneness where we have been led to know that we are never alone;
   For the companionship of Thy presence in judgment and grace, the closeness of Thy "no" and of Thy "yes";
   For every sign of Thy Spirit's quest for us that turns our darkness into light;
   For all Thy tender ministries when we have heard Thee call us by our name to be fully Thy children,

> We thank Thee, Lord.

   For insights bestowed through the disappointment of low and base ambitions;
   For every revelation vouchsafed amid personal failures:
      Help us to see and feel Thy creative intention.

For the benediction of new beginnings;
For the healing ministry of time that casts the gentle veil of her forgetfulness upon the scars of long ago;
For the sweet service of memory that preserves indelible the precious blessings of yesterdays long gone to inspire the ambitions of today;
For all that leads us to receive strength in the day of our weakness, light amid our darkness, and life in the presence of death.

> For these and all Thy blessings,
> We thank Thee, our Father.

>> Amen.

A Prayer for Deliverance from Debasing Fears

> From all false imaginings that lead us to believe that living is more dangerous than in fact it is;
> From all indulgence in the world of frightened make-believe;
> From all morbid exaggerations of our past sins;
> From every attempt to empty life of its resources, to take refuge in selfish despair, and to enjoy the deadliness of self-pity:

From all such, raise us anew through the sweet ministries of Thy Holy Spirit to the glad assurance of Thy transfiguring Grace, so that we become more than conquerors through Him that loved us and gave Himself for us that our joy might be full.

> So let this be, O Lord.

Amen.

A Prayer for Daily Guidance (III)

Eternal God, who dost ever call those who serve Thee to the labors of a new day, help us to greet the tasks which the days may lay upon us with faithful commitment.

Save us from littleness of heart and pettiness of spirit, lest we add to the woes of the world.

Deliver us in all our ways from becoming little men in large places, false men in high places, or timid souls in the hour of high opportunity.

Do Thou so gird our lives with the inspiration of Thy Holy Spirit that we may always adorn and never belittle the stations to which Thou hast called us one by one.

Teach us so to number our days that we may apply our hearts to wisdom and our minds and strength to the work of our time, thus bringing to the counsels of this age the truth of the Ages.

Through Jesus Christ, our Lord,

Amen.

A Prayer for a New Year (II)

Gracious and Eternal God, as we stand upon the threshold between the Old and the New, in this hour of new beginnings, awaken in us a thankful heart for Thy gracious ministry whereby we have been brought to this moment:

As we enter upon the responsibilities and privileges of the coming days, strengthen us to live as those who have been awakened to the urgency of living, as those who would always adorn and never belittle the station with which Thou hast entrusted us.

Through Jesus Christ, our Lord,

Amen.

A Prayer for Daily Guidance (IV)

Almighty God, in knowledge of whom standeth our Eternal life, grant us the courage to fulfill the tasks which the days may bring forth.

Enable us to find in work well done, and in faithfulness to little duties that serenity of mind and heart which is our true health.

From all divisions between desire and duty, between love of self and love of Thee, save us by Thy Grace to a glad acceptance of Thy Spirit's leading in all our ways,

Through Jesus Christ, our Lord,

Amen.

**A Prayer for the Grace
to Strengthen Others**

From all unwitting mutilation of our fellows by careless word, or deliberate slander;

From all in us that makes it harder for others to succeed;

From all oversight of the consequence of our weakness upon those who, without our knowing it, have taken us for their ladders to the noble and the good;

From everything in us that makes for the ghastly possibility that through our life and example others may have been led to surrender their dream or to fall in the hour of their testing;

    Deliver us, we beseech Thee.

    Help me to answer Thee, O Lord, with my life.

                           Amen.

A Thanksgiving Prayer

For the marvels of Thy constancy amid our wayward disobedience;

For every token within the common round of daily tasks when we have felt the gentle strength of Thy quest for our souls;

For the evidence that Thou hast entered the life of our world, that here Thou hast addressed us one by one, and that our history bears the mark of Thy habitation in our midst:

                We thank Thee, our Father.

For all that leads to find that in our fleeting pilgrimage Thou hast set the mark of Thine Eternity; in our darkness the presence of Thy Light; amid our weakness Thy strength; and in our silence Thine Eternal Word:

For these and all Thy Mercies, enable us to be truly thankful, O Lord.

    Amen.

Two Vesper Prayers

As the day ebbs to its close, and in the darkening sky the stars come out, and a hush descends upon the fret-filled day, even so, let Thy coming to our Spirits be.

Awaken us to the wholesome ministry of reflection and converse with Thee, and through the same to the sure knowledge that Thou, O Lord, alone art the true home of our souls.

Even so, let it be, we pray Thee.

Amen.

* * *

Forgive, our Father, the folly of our ways:

For deep and serious sins of faithlessness and insincerity that have embittered the sweetness of life;

For the vain hope that has thought to gain success without cost, achievement without sweat;

For all our misconceivings of the life of the Spirit, we pray Thy forgiveness and the transfiguring power of Thy Holy Spirit.

Through Jesus Christ, our Lord,

Amen.

A Prayer for Daily Strength

From all negligence of our responsibility to others;

From all contentment with the betterment of our lot at the expense of those less fortunate than we;

From all inconsistencies of life that frustrate in our time the doing of Thy will;

From laziness that is content to let others carry out our duties; entertains only narrow horizons and low ambitions;

From all in us that makes Thy Church to be scorned because of the blasphemy of our pale imitations of Thy Grace and Truth;

From all such, deliver us, we pray Thee, by the renewing of our minds and hearts,

Through the power of Thy Holy Spirit,

                                                Amen.

**A Prayer in Thanksgiving
for Love and Friendship**

We thank Thee, O Lord, for the gift of life in a society of men and women, of young and the aged, boys and girls:

    For the wondrous gifts of friendship and love;
        of marriage and parenthood;
        of houses blessed with new images of Thy
            likeness in which our own are entwined;
    For the blessings of shared intimacies,
        of disciplines undergone,
        of lessons learned, and new achievements attained;
    For all the wonders of growing up in stature of
        body and spirit—
    For every blessing from Thy hand so freely and fully
        given, we thank Thee, O Lord.

Let Thy presence so guide us that we may know the sacredness of life unbelittled, the beauty of trust unbetrayed, and the joy of spirit unspoiled, because Thou dost rule the inner citadel of our being.

                Through Jesus Christ, our Lord,

                                Amen.

A Prayer for the World's Workers

We beseech Thy Providence and Grace for all who labor in their several and particular stations in this world's life:

We pray for all who are pressed by the cares and beset by the temptations of business life;

When we are tempted in the struggle for food and raiment, housing and salary, to seek much more than our needs for the day, teach us to acknowledge before Thee our common guilt for the hardness and deceit that we have caused to exist in every area of human relations.

Grant us a heart to repent and the will to transform all the structures of human relationship so that righteousness and peace shall reign among the communities of men and nations.

Grant us to live with one another

in peace and harmony,

in love and justice,

O Lord,

Amen.

Commencement Prayers

I

Thou who art the Author, the Giver, and the Sustainer of the truth we seek, enrich, we beseech Thee, the splendor of this moment with the inspiration of Thy Presence and the power of Thy Living Touch.

In this moment when the new milestone for many of us is fraught with the significance of objectives now attained, of success in the quest for Truth, and of true happiness and joy in our victory, grant that in this same moment that humility may be ours which belongs to all who know they are learners. May the attainments of the present moment not blind us to the challenge that yet lies before us, in the great continents of the unknown.

Bless, with the continual sense of Thy Presence, those to whom is entrusted the task of leadership and instruction of new minds. May all dogmatism, pride of mind, and conceit be unknown to them; undergird with the pulse of Truth's Living Touch all those who sit in the seats of the learners. Endow them with the simplicity that is not afraid of facts; with the humble recognition that we do but tread the outer fringe of Thy thoughts after Thee in this mysterious Universe.

To all who share tonight the joys and the attainments of this victorious hour, grant them true happiness in the knowledge that they are equipped to serve not themselves, but the needs of a waiting and needy generation in the service of unselfish devotion.

May this prayer be truly our own.

Amen.

II

Gracious and Eternal God, who art the author of our Spirits, and in whose gracious providence we live and move and have our being, bless, we pray Thee, this day of our human exultations with the inspiration of Thy Living Presence.

As we stand tonight at the turning of the road, where the hosts that have preceded us have stood before us, in this happy hour of our endings and of our "new" beginnings, grant unto us a heart of thankfulness for all the gracious ministry whereby we have been brought to this high moment, when we shall be sealed afresh as the new sons and daughters of this community of minds and hearts, our university. Let the remembrance of the zest and happiness of these years here fall as a benediction upon all our days.

As now we bid farewell, enable us to take our place in the life and work of the world as those who have been awakened to the urgency of living; as those who would be worthy of the privilege which has been theirs; as those who now shall go seeking not to be ministered unto, but to minister.

To the inspiration and significance of all that is symbolized in this deep and searching hour, help us to be faithful throughout the coming days,

Through Jesus Christ, our Lord,

Amen.

A Prayer for Convocation Day

Almighty and Everlasting God, who art the Light of the minds that know Thee, the Life of the souls that love Thee, and the Strength of the wills that serve Thee, let Thy gracious benediction rest, we pray Thee, upon this day of our "new beginnings."

To those who return to take up their work in this place, let this hour be as the deepening of an old friendship with strenuous tasks and high responsibility for the goodly gifts from the gracious hand of Life.

To those who come into our midst for the first time, let this moment be the open door through which they enter into the light of a new and greater day. Grant, we pray Thee, that the high resolves and inspiration of this hour may not wane, nor their ambitions waver in days when the road is steep and the pathway long and hard.

Unto us all, give, we beseech Thee, such openness of mind, simpleness of heart, and sincerity of spirit that we may live as becometh those who, having looked into the face of the glad mystery of life, have been delivered alike from the stubborn rejection of new truth, and from the hasty assumption that we are wiser than our fathers.

To the inspiration and significance of this and the succeeding days, help us to be true.

        Through Jesus Christ,

                Amen.